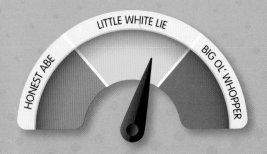

REAL

OR

FAKE? ③

EVEN MORE
FAR-OUT FIBS, FISHY FACTS,
AND PHONY PHOTOS
TO TEST FOR THE TRUTH

EMILY KRIEGER
ILLUSTRATIONS BY TOM NICK COCOTOS

NATIONAL GEOGRAPHIC
WASHINGTON, D.C.

CONTENTS

Welcome to
REAL OR FAKE? 3

the book where you get to **TEST YOUR INNER LIE DETECTOR!** Before you dive in, let's go over the basics of sorting a fact from a fib.

How do you identify a lie? Sometimes it's hard to put your finger on a fake, but here are a few clues to help you along the way:

IT'S ALL IN THE DETAILS

Be on the lookout for details in a story that are inconsistent, or just seem impossible. Also, people have a tendency to overexplain when they're feeling guilty about something; likewise, some details in these stories just aren't necessary. Sometimes that can be a key identifier in figuring out where the truth is stretched.

USE YOUR NOGGIN

If things in the story don't exactly line up with things you know to be true, go with what you know. Experience is one of the best teachers in life, so use yours when trying to determine what is real and what is fake.

GO WITH YOUR GUT

If things seem too unbelievable to be true, oftentimes they are. Trust your instincts when things seem off—a good rule for this book and in life!

WHAT'S A FIB-O-METER? A fib-o-meter is a handy little gauge we've invented for determining the level of a lie (or truth). The categories are Honest Abe, Little White Lie, and Big Ol' Whopper. We've gone through and determined which story falls where based on whether it's true or how big a lie it is. If the story is true, it falls in Honest Abe territory. If the details of the story are untrue and the lie is minor, we've gone with Little White Lie. If it was a big lie that maybe led to something else (widespread panic or disbelief, maybe), we've gone with Big Ol' Whopper. Agree with our findings? Decide for yourself as you rate things on the fib-o-meter!

FULL STOMACH
CAUSES SNEEZING

The human body has weird glitches. One example: When a person becomes so full after a meal they start sneezing uncontrollably. The phenomenon is called snatiation. The word is a play on two others: sneeze and satiate, which means "full." And though some people may sometimes sneeze after a meal, snatiators (as they're called) *always* sneeze, between 3 and 15 times in a row, after a meal so big they can't take another bite. And it doesn't matter what type of food they eat. Or what time of day they eat. Snatiation was first reported in 1989, by doctors in Kuwait who noticed the trait among members of a family. Since then, snatiators around the world have spoken up, amused to now have a name for the harmless quirk.

REAL

HONEST ABE

SNATIATORS OF THE WORLD, UNITE! SCIENTISTS AREN'T EXACTLY SURE WHY SOME PEOPLE SNEEZE UNCONTROLLABLY WHEN FULL. But they have a good guess: The neurons that control sneezing are very close to the neurons that control digestion.

11

PIGEONS PUT ON
LIGHT SHOW

REAL OR FAKE?

New York City is known as the home to some superfamous stars. But look up, and it's clear that it's also home to a huge pigeon population, which many people consider pests. But one artist begs to differ: He and his pigeon pals created an aerial show that anyone would say is amazing. To put on the performance, the artist attached tiny, remote-controlled LED lights to bird leg bands. Then he trained thousands of pigeons living aboard a ship to take to the air when he blew a whistle at dusk. What happened after the pigeons took flight was unrehearsed. The birds' swooping movements through the night sky created a starry show that viewers said resembled fireworks or a sea of shooting stars! The birds performed both as a group and solo, becoming artists themselves for a half hour each evening before being signaled back to the ship.

The performance pigeons lived not far from where the U.S. Navy housed its first fleet of messenger pigeons, or birds trained to CARRY SECRET MESSAGES DURING WARTIME!

REAL

HONEST
ABE

THIS FREE PERFORMANCE PIECE, TITLED "FLY BY NIGHT," RAN FOR SIX WEEKENDS IN SPRING 2016. The birds stayed in 13 custom-built coops on an old ship docked in the Brooklyn Navy Yard. The artist who put on the show, Duke Riley, said he did so to pay tribute to the city, its famous pigeons, and the people who keep and train the birds, called pigeon fanciers.

DEATH VALLEY'S UNDERGROUND CITY

Death Valley, California, U.S.A., is home to the hottest temperatures on Earth. Anything that lives there has to be hardy and able to withstand extreme heat. The town of Ovendale sits in the valley's center, but if you look for it, you might miss it. That's because the entire city lies 300 feet (91 m) below the scorching desert surface! In 1862, two explorers used dynamite to create a deep-down maze of tunnels and turned them into streets for some 7,000 people (and their pets!). Homes are simple squares with earthen walls. The same goes for the 22 businesses belowground, including a popular grocery store chain that just moved in (or is it under?). Why would people choose to live underground? It's the only way to survive Death Valley year-round, says Ovendale's mayor. And the valley, with its unique extremes, is the only place the town's residents ever want to call home.

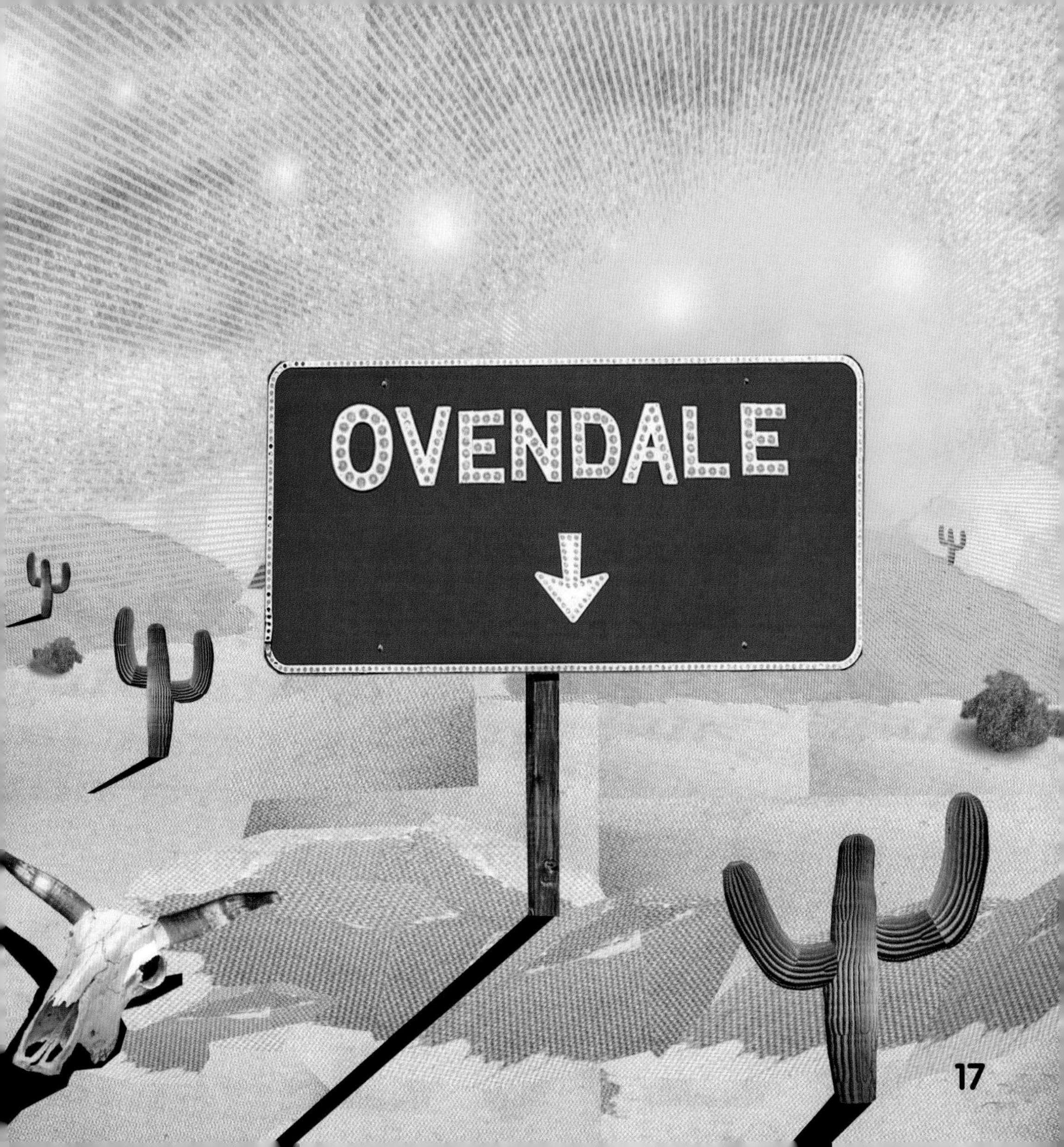
OVENDALE

FAKE!

LITTLE WHITE LIE

THERE IS NO OVENDALE, NOR ANY HUMAN POPULATION THAT LIVES SO DEEP IN THE EARTH.

The real Australian town of Coober Pedy comes closest, though: About half its 3,500 residents live beneath the desert (at most some 50 feet [15 m] down) or in homes built into hillsides. People can live, eat, work, swim, visit museums, and even attend religious services underground! The town was built by opal miners in the early 20th century looking to escape the area's extreme heat.

INVENTIONS

They say necessity is the mother of invention, but it's hard to believe people saw a need for these crazy creations! Check out the products below and decide which of these wild wares are REAL, and which are just the figment of a WILD imagination.

1 LEGO-HAIR BIKE HELMET

2 DEVICE THAT TRANSLATES DOG BARKS INTO CAT MEOWS

3 UMBRELLA THAT ALERTS YOUR PHONE WHEN IT'S GOING TO RAIN

4 FITNESS TRACKER FOR DOGS

5 A GARBAGE CAN THAT TAKES ITSELF OUT TO THE CURB ON COMMAND

6 TOWEL THAT LOOKS LIKE A TORTILLA

ANSWERS: 1. Real; 2. Fake; 3. Real; 4. Real; 5. Fake; 6. Real

21

SCULPTURES AT THE BOTTOM OF THE SEA

Imagine snorkeling off the coast of Cancún, Mexico, and seeing not only fish and sea turtles but also hundreds of people sitting, standing, watching TV, and eating on the seafloor! That's exactly what you'd find at the Underwater Museum of Art, 12 to 27 feet (3.5 to 8 m) deep in the Caribbean Sea. Though the people aren't real—they're statues—they are life-size and lifelike and posed in everyday activities, alongside cars and houses and other items, too. Some of the sculptures are a little eerie, such as the heads sticking out of a bed of seaweed and a circle of giant hands. But all of the art has an awesome purpose: It's made from material that promotes coral growth and acts as an artificial reef. So visitors—who view the museum by glass-bottomed boat, snorkel, or scuba—can admire not only the art but also the many types of marine life it attracts!

22

MUSEUM

TICKET 194359

HONEST ABE

REAL

THE UNDERWATER MUSEUM OF ART OFF MEXICO'S YUCATÁN PENINSULA OPENED IN 2009 TO BOTH PROMOTE AND PROTECT MARINE LIFE. Since then, coral and algae have anchored themselves to the art, while creatures from fish to lobsters to sea turtles swim among the more than 500 sculptures spread across the seafloor. This cool collection of undersea art and nature isn't the only one of its kind: The first underwater art museum opened in 2006 off the island of Grenada in the Caribbean.

CORN FUNGUS
GETS FANCY TREATMENT

If you ever shuck an ear of corn and find it covered in gray fungus, don't throw it away—that freaky find is a delicacy! So say some people in Mexico, where the fungus grows on corn from August through October. Called *cuitlacoche* (queet-la-coh-chay), it swells and rots kernels until they resemble squishy rocks. When cooked, it turns into a dark, tar-like sludge that fans say has an earthy, mushroom-like flavor. Most corn farmers in the United States will toss an ear if the fungus has fouled even one kernel. Millions of dollars have been spent trying to wipe out the fungus in America. But in Mexico, people forage for the fungus to sell at markets and to chefs to put in everything from tacos to tamales to soups. Even the ancient Aztec ate cuitlacoche!

FUN FACT

Human feet are home to about 80 TO 100 DIFFERENT TYPES OF FUNGUS. The heel is the most populated part of the foot.

REAL

HONEST ABE

ALSO CALLED CORN SMUT, CUITLACOCHE HAS A FAN BASE THAT'S GROWING IN BOTH SIZE AND LOCATION. Some U.S. farmers are now harvesting the fungus when they find it on their crops and selling it to chefs at fancy American restaurants. And a few U.S. scientists are even perfecting how to infect corn crops on purpose!

WACKY HEADLINES

Extra! Extra! Read all about it! Some of the headlines below are totally made-up, but some have actually been published. Read on to see if you can determine which are the FAKES.

1 PEOPLE KNOWINGLY DONATED $100,000 TO DIG A BIG, POINTLESS HOLE IN THE GROUND

2 SCIENTISTS USE SUNLIGHT TO TURN FOOTBALL INTO BASKETBALL

3 REINDEER MAY DITCH PRESENTS, DELIVER PIZZA

4 TARANTULAS MAY BE "RIGHT-HANDED"

WHATEVER

5 "WHATEVER" IS THE **MOST ANNOYING WORD** FOR THE EIGHTH YEAR IN A ROW

6 IDAHO MAN USES **WARM BREATH** TO FREE SPARROW WITH FEET FROZEN TO METAL PIPE

7 CHEF INVENTS **TALKING CHEESEBURGER**

8 AMAZING **OLD-MAN DISGUISE** HELPED 31-YEAR-OLD FUGITIVE EVADE COPS FOR MONTHS

9 MINNESOTA SISTERS PLAY **GAME OF CHASE** FOR 47 DAYS, OVER 222 MILES (357 KM)

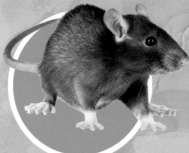

10 POLICE SEEK **TUTU BANDIT** IN FLORIDA

11 RATS ARE **TICKLISH**, SOMETIMES

ANSWERS: 2, 7, and 9 are fake.

31

TODDLER TICKETED FOR LITTERING

In 2016, a $75 ticket for littering made national news—because it was issued to a two-year-old! A Washington, D.C., city official unknowingly issued the ticket to the toddler after finding mail addressed to the kid along with the litter. The official assumed the name on the envelope pointed to the culprit's identity. After receiving the ticket, the kid's parents thought a quick call to the official to explain would sort things out. But no—even after being told the ticket had been issued to a toddler, the official still refused to tear it up! So the parents posted their silly story on the Internet. A lot of people ended up reading it and thought it was outrageous that a two-year-old was being fined. Eventually the public outcry became so strong that the toddler's ticket was finally thrown out—a victory for common sense.

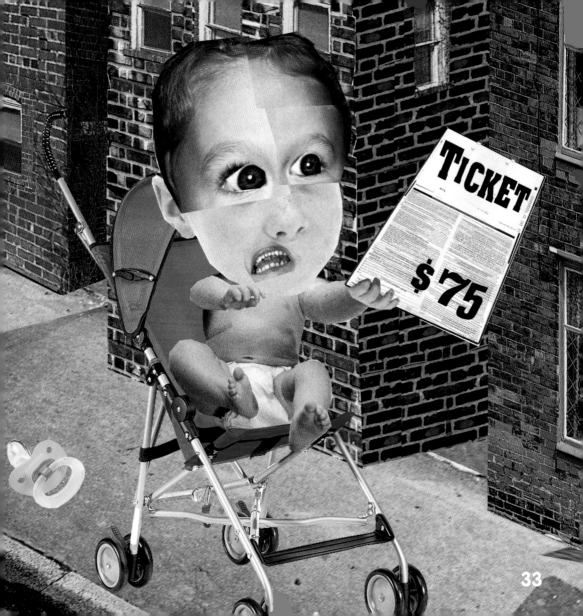

REAL

HONEST ABE

IT'S ROUGH OUT THERE WHEN TODDLERS ARE GETTING TICKETS! Not only was the toddler's mom ticked that her kid got a ticket, she also argued that a piece of mail found with the trash wasn't enough evidence to accuse someone. When a reporter asked the toddler where she had been at the time of the crime, she laughed and said, "Hide-and-seek."

A toddler getting a ticket made news in 2012, too. That time, a three-year-old got a $2,500 TICKET FOR URINATING IN PUBLIC! That ticket, too, was torn up after public outcry.

SPOT THE FAKE!

Do you have the eye of a spy? See if you can tell which of these photos are REAL and which are really FAKE!

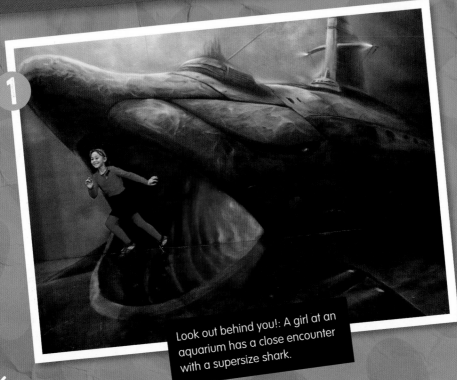

Look out behind you!: A girl at an aquarium has a close encounter with a supersize shark.

1

2

Little-known fact: A strong blast of air can blow off a Dalmatian's black dots.

SPOT THE FAKE!

①

When the reindeer get too tired, sometimes Santa has to turn to an unlikely animal: a T. rex!

2

It takes a lot of effort for an elephant to balance on an itty-bitty scooter.

BIG PIGS
OVERRUN ISLAND

REAL OR FAKE?

The tiny French island of Emore, in the Atlantic Ocean, has a big population problem. But it doesn't involve people. It's a big pig problem—specifically, some 2,000 pot-bellied pigs have made the island their home and sent its few human inhabitants fleeing! In 2012, about a dozen farmers on the island reported that a trickster had opened pigpens overnight, letting loose hundreds of the animals. Trying to round them up proved problematic, with each pig weighing in at 100-plus pounds (45 kg). Within a few days, herds of porkers had rooted their way across the island, destroying farmland as they went and freaking out the farmers. The French government declared a state of emergency, but rather than try to save the island from the pigs, the government handed it over to them. Since then, it's been a pig paradise!

FUN FACT

A small island off the west coast of Canada is home to dozens of SAINT BERNARD DOGS. Packs roam the woods off-leash, but are still under the care of humans!

FAKE!

BIG OL' WHOPPER

THE STORY OF THOUSANDS OF REALLY BIG PIGS TAKING OVER THE ISLAND OF EMORE (WHICH DOESN'T EXIST) IS MADE-UP. But this tale isn't terribly far from the truth: Some small islands host big populations of animals, such as "cat islands" in Japan and New York; a Puerto Rican island overrun by monkeys; and even a Caribbean island that's home to pigs—but 20, not 2,000!

IDENTIFY THE LIE!

For each question group below, two statements are TRUE, and one is FALSE. Can you put your finger on the fib?

1

A. In the Netherlands in the 17th century, a single tulip cost as much as a horse.

B. Otters weighing more than 100 pounds (45 kg) roamed what is now China six million years ago.

C. A donkey danced for a Russian ballet company for 19 years.

44

2

A. At an opera house that straddles the U.S.–Canada border, the stage is in Quebec, but many of the seats are in Vermont!

B. Dung beetles don't get lost thanks to an extraordinary ability to memorize tiny details in the dirt.

C. Cats can be allergic to people.

ANSWERS: 1. A: A 17th-century tulip cost even more—as much as a luxury home! Historians have a word for this freaky flower phase: *Tulpenwoede*, which means "tulip madness." 2. B: Dung beetles have an amazing memory, but it's for what's above, not below them. Scientists studying the insects found they navigate by memorizing the positions of the sun, moon, and stars.

APP MAKES LUNCHTIME
LESS SCARY

REAL OR FAKE?

Scanning the school lunchroom for a place to sit can stink. So a teen figured out a way to make the everyday ritual a little less scary. She invented an app called Sit With Us that lets users find friendly people to sit with. They can register as "ambassadors" and post "open lunches," which welcome anyone to the table, or just log in and search for nearby seatmates to join. And users can chat with each other through the app, to make plans or simply say hi. The California teen created the app after eating alone her entire seventh grade year, which she said made her a target for bullying. The app helps kids find safe people to sit with, without anyone other than them knowing the match was made online. And, it's free!

REAL

THE LUNCH BUDDY APP SIT WITH US WAS LAUNCHED BY 16-YEAR-OLD NATALIE HAMPTON IN SEPTEMBER 2016, JUST IN TIME FOR THE START OF SCHOOL THAT YEAR. Though the Sherman Oaks teen says her social life is much better now, the memory of those middle school years inspired her to try to help others.

49

DUMPSTER DIVE

Talk about a party pooper: **Residents of a city block in Philadelphia, Pennsylvania, U.S.A.,** made national news after they filled a Dumpster with water and used it as a pool! It sounds gross, but a lot of people got in, and even ate while bobbing up and down on floaties. Perhaps their fears were eased by the fact that the party's organizers had power-washed the Dumpster, and then lined it with plywood and tarps before filling it with water. But where the water came from was the biggest problem with the party. It was taken from a nearby fire hydrant, without permission and without common sense, city officials said. Using water intended for fires instead for a pool just isn't cool. And the flow from the hydrant can be strong enough to seriously injure someone. The penalty for these partygoers? No more parties on their block—ever!

FUN FACT

The largest pool in the world, in Algarrobo, Chile, is more than 20 times the length of an Olympic swimming pool and holds 66 MILLION GALLONS (250 million L) of water!

52

REAL

HONEST ABE

THIS BIZARRE BASH HAPPENED IN SUMMER 2016. As photos of the party appeared on social media, the story spread, and city officials quickly cracked down on Dumpster pool parties. Philadelphians got creative, though, and the next weekend held pool parties in the beds of pickup trucks!

LOADING LEVEL
LOAD ABOVE TOP

IDENTIFY THE LIE!

For each question group below,
two statements are TRUE, and one is FALSE.
Can you put your finger on the fib?

The game that ties you up in knots!
Twister

Kids   AGE 6+   2 PLAYERS 10   ADULT ASSEMBLY REQUIRED.

1

A. The game Twister was originally called Pretzel.

B. It's impossible to surf a river.

C. There's a travel agency that provides vacations for stuffed animals.

2

A. The record for most pairs of underpants put on in one hour is 144, set by a U.K. man in 2009.

B. It costs half a cent to make a penny.

C. It took 20,000 workers 22 years to build the Taj Mahal, in India.

ANSWERS: 1. B: You can hang ten on the Amazon River thanks to a natural phenomenon called a tidal bore, when a wave from the ocean travels upstream. Surfers ride waves up to 12 feet (3.6 m) tall! 2. B: It costs about 1.5 cents to make a penny, or more than the coin is worth! The metals pennies are made from have become more expensive in recent years.

CAT LOVER
BY A WHISKER

Sometimes you aren't sure about adding another pet to the family. Will the animals' personalities be a good fit? There's a crazy-sounding, simple way to predict at least one thing: Whether a dog likes cats. Amazingly, the answer to this question lies in the number of whiskers on a dog's snout. Dogs with an even number (such as 2, 4, 6, 8—any number divisible by 2) are fans of felines. Dogs with an odd number (3, 5, 7, 9, etc.) can't stand 'em. It's hard to get a dog to stay still long enough to count its whiskers. (Tip: A good time to try this is while your dog is asleep!) But taking a little time to count whiskers could save everyone a whole lot of heartache later.

FAKE!

BIG OL' WHOPPER

THIS TWITCHY-SOUNDING TALE IS A TALL ONE! BUT A LOT OF PEOPLE PROBABLY WISH IT WERE TRUE. It'd be convenient to be able to tell whether a dog likes cats by doing a whisker count. But whiskers can predict other cool things. Animals use them to help feel their way around the world and tell, for example, whether their bodies will be able to fit into a space. And look closely: Whiskers don't grow only on snouts. They also grow above the eyes and on chins!

AT EARTH'S CENTER:
ANOTHER EARTH?!

Deep down in the center of Earth is something really weird: another, ancient planet! The cold, rocky sphere scientists call proto-Earth (proto means "original" or "primitive") is a little-known secret nestled more than a thousand miles (1,600 km) beneath people's feet. First discovered in 1975, its existence has been called into question repeatedly by earth scientists who couldn't believe it—until they had the evidence in hand, in 2007. That year, researchers in Morocco announced that by studying seismic waves (the ones that cause earthquakes) and chemicals drilled from Earth's core, they had proof that a roughly Mars-size old Earth was lodged in the center of our planet. They estimate it's more than 20 billion years old. Because it's so cold, they don't believe it's home to any life. But to be sure, plans are in place to send machines to study the planet, as soon as 2045.

FUN FACT

People have also posited that the CENTER OF EARTH IS HOLLOW, filled with dinosaurs, and liquid.

FAKE!

BIG OL' WHOPPER

THERE'S A LOT WRONG WITH THIS FAR-OUT STORY ABOUT A PLANET WITHIN A PLANET.

The center of Earth is a very hot, solid, metal core that's slightly smaller than the moon (which is about half the size of Mars). Surrounding that is a liquid layer of metal. And the proto-planet couldn't be 20 billion years old—the universe is only 13.7 billion years old. The word "proto" (which is real) may have thrown you off. But don't be fooled by fancy words: Fakers use them, too, and sometimes even make them up!

ONE PRICEY POTTY

Is an 18-karat-gold toilet a work of art? Beauty is in the eye of the beholder, but New York City's Guggenheim Museum says yes. In 2016, it became the home of a working toilet cast in gold, created by famed Italian artist Maurizio Cattelan. Visitors are encouraged to touch the art—*really* touch it. The very pretty potty, located in a fifth-floor bathroom, can be used like any ordinary toilet. But first, flushers have to listen to a short lecture about the art from a security guard stationed outside. The toilet needs TLC when it comes to cleaning. Every 15 minutes an employee wipes it down. Less often, it receives a steam cleaning. And, if you're wondering, the commode comes with only everyday accessories—no gold tissue!

REAL

HONEST
ABE

TALK ABOUT A ROYAL FLUSH! Why would somebody make a gold toilet? Cattelan explains he wanted to offer museumgoers an opportunity typically reserved only for the very wealthy. Fans have been flocking to the throne, and the museum has no plans to replace it anytime soon.

FUN FACT

Artist MARCEL DUCHAMP caused a stir in 1917 when he unveiled his artwork titled "Fountain"—a urinal with his signature on it!

IDENTIFY THE LIE!

For each question group below, two statements are TRUE, and one is FALSE. Can you put your finger on the fib?

1

A. The U.S. Library of Congress has 268 miles (431 km) of bookshelves.

B. The first Olympic athletes competed nude.

C. Bill Clinton was the first U.S. president to ever send an email.

2

A. Opossums don't "play dead"—they actually pass out from fear.

B. A horny toad is actually a snake.

C. Coydogs are hybrid canines in which one parent is a coyote, the other a dog.

ANSWERS: 1. A: The Library of Congress, the largest library in the world, is home to more than 164 million items on about 838 miles (1,350 km) of bookshelves! It adds about 12,000 items to its collections every day! 2. B: Though a horny toad's face and torso resemble a toad, in truth it's a lizard. It also goes by the name short-horned lizard.

THE BOY WHO THOUGHT HE WAS A KANGAROO

REAL OR FAKE?

What has two legs and bounces? A boy raised by kangaroos! In 2014, reports of a wild child living among the marsupials began pouring into Australia's remote Office of Outback Wildlife. Ranchers said they'd seen a boy, estimated to be about 10 years old, hopping on his legs and grooming and eating with a group of about a dozen red kangaroos. Several of the ranchers called out to the boy, but he seemed to not understand English. Instead, he reared his head back and made a strange, high-pitched sound and bounced away. The ranchers say the boy appears to be healthy and even happy: On a few occasions, he was seen playing with younger kangaroos, pretending to punch one another in the arm!

FAKE!

LITTLE WHITE LIE

STORIES ABOUT A BOY LIVING WITH KANGAROOS CAN BE FOUND ONLINE, BUT THEY'RE MADE-UP. As are many other stories about feral, or wild, children discovered living among all sorts of animals from monkeys to wolves. One of the oldest such stories is the legend of Romulus and Remus, the twin boys who founded Rome and were said to be rescued from a river and fed by a wolf and a woodpecker.

73

STUDENTS STRIKE OVER HOMEWORK

In 2016, millions of students in Spain refused to do their home-work for the entire month of November. But they didn't get in trouble. Fed up with how much time they spend on homework—6.5 hours a week on average—they went on strike—with their parents' support! Both kids and adults agreed homework had gotten out of hand. So the country's parents association advised kids to stop doing their after-school assignments, in the hopes that the school system would cut back. Some teachers gave students lower grades for failure to turn in homework. But other teachers sympathized with the students and started assigning less. The strikers considered those cutbacks—and the worldwide reporting on the issue—a success and decided to stay sans homework during December, too!

FUN FACT

FUN FACT
Students in Shanghai, China, spend the most time on homework: 14 HOURS A WEEK on average. Students in Finland and Korea spend the least: less than 3 hours a week.

HONEST
ABE

REAL

IT MAY SEEM LIKE A DREAM, BUT STUDENTS AND PARENTS IN SPAIN REALLY DID TAKE A STAND AGAINST HOMEWORK IN LATE 2016.

Parents explained that although homework keeps kids busy after school, their grades don't reflect all their hard work. Compared with kids in other countries, Spanish students do more homework but still score below average in science, math, and reading. Something's not adding up, say the strikers, and the system needs to change.

77

BATSQUATCH!

Poor Batsquatch. Most people have never heard of the creepy creature. The better-known Sasquatch (aka Bigfoot) always steals the spotlight. But some people say Batsquatch is the more fearsome of the two—because it flies! Imagine a bat that's 9 feet (3 m) tall with leathery wings as wide as a road, bluish fur, and a face like a wolf. That's what a man swore he saw land about 30 feet (9 m) ahead of him one night in 1994 near Washington, U.S.A.'s Mount Rainier. His encounter was reported in a local newspaper, Tacoma's *News Tribune*. In 2009, two hikers near Mount Shasta, California, reported seeing a similar creature take flight. They estimated its wingspan to be even bigger, about 50 feet (15 m)! Nobody knows where Batsquatch will turn up next, but believers are hoping someone will snap a photo of it soon.

LITTLE WHITE LIE

BATSQUATCH AND SASQUATCH HAVE MORE IN COMMON THAN JUST THEIR NAMES. They're also not real. The region where people have reported seeing them, the U.S. Pacific Northwest, is famous for its freaky fake creatures, including the tree octopus, which appeared in the first book of this series. Scientists say that without evidence such as bones, hair, or teeth to study, it's impossible to confirm these creatures exist.

81

FISH FIGHT!

When people think of fearsome animals found in the water, sharks, snakes, and alligators come to mind. But did you know there's a 20-pound (9-kg) fish that flings itself out of water and whacks boaters so hard they fall overboard? Called silver carp, the fish from Asia arrived in American lakes, rivers, and streams by accident (a few escaped from farms) in the 1970s. Their big appetites mean less food for native fish species, putting those populations at risk. And the carp have become a threat to people, too—by literally leaping out of the water and smacking them so hard they're sent to the hospital with bloody noses and broken bones! People have even reported being knocked out by them! Officials and scientists say silver carp have got to go. Their solution? They say people need to start eating the fish, which are a popular food in Asia.

84

REAL

HONEST ABE

LOOK OUT! This story may sound fishy, but silver carp really do leap out of the water and whack boaters so hard they've sent them to the hospital! These fish aren't looking for a fight, though. They fling themselves out of the water because they're startled by the sound of approaching motorboats.

SPOT THE FAKE!

Do you have the eye of a spy? See if you can tell which of these photos are REAL and which are really FAKE!

Unicorns aren't real, but Pegasuses do exist!

1

2

A kangaroo checks into a really wild Australian hotel that allows only animals as guests!

1

Dogs can do anything, including ride the waves atop a boogie board!

2

This silly scene had onlookers crying laughing, too.

An alligator and a butterfly can be best friends ... but only for a few seconds (snap!).

1

This kid played Minecraft one too many times and got permanently stuck in character.

DOCTORS GROW
AN EYE ON A CHEEK

In 2015, doctors in South Africa announced the unthinkable: They grew an eye on a man's cheek! The weird science wasn't just for show. It was an effort to provide the patient—a 29-year-old who had lost his left eye in a fishing accident—with a replacement peeper. While the wound where his old eye had been healed, doctors used cells from the man's right, still working eye to grow an eye in a petri dish. After 57 days, the eye had matured enough to be put on the man's cheek, where it gave his body a chance to adjust to the foreign part. By opening and closing his mouth, the man can open and shut the eye. But he can't see anything out of it—yet. Doctors hope that after several more surgeries it will be a working eye that can then be put in its proper place.

FAKE!

BIG OL' WHOPPER

THIS FREAKY STORY IS FAKE.

An eye is too complex a body part (it's literally connected to your brain) to grow elsewhere on the body and still function. Maybe one day in the future doctors will be able to do this. But for now, they can do something similar and still very cool: In 2013, doctors in China used cartilage from a patient's rib to grow a new nose for him on his forehead! They selected that spot because from there it would be easiest to move the nose to its new home.

CAT-CRAZY
EGYPTIANS

People can be nuts about their pets, with some even joking that they worship them. But more than 2,500 years ago, ancient Egyptians really did. They built a beautiful temple where people worshipped the goddess Bastet, who was a cat! And not only were they nuts about her, they were nuts about all cats. The Egyptians held elaborate ceremonies in Bastet's honor and filled her temple with thousands of carved cat statues. They dressed their cats in real jewels, fed them fancy food, and wore cat charms as part of their everyday attire. When a cat died, it was mummified and buried with a few of its favorite things, such as milk and mice. And the cat's caretakers shaved off their eyebrows to show how upset they were. If the cat had died at the hands of a human, even accidentally, that person had a far worse fate: The punishment for killing any cat ever was death.

REAL

HONEST
ABE

ANCIENT EGYPTIANS REALLY WERE CRAZY ABOUT CATS! THE CENTER OF WORSHIP FOR CAT LOVERS WAS A CITY CALLED PER-BAST, IN NORTHERN EGYPT. There, believers built a temple to honor Bastet, a goddess who could appear as a cat, a lioness, or a woman with a cat's head. Historians say the cat craze could have started when Egyptians noticed the animals were good at catching vermin and so encouraged them to hang around.

FUN FACT

The ancient Egyptians' word for cat SOUNDED LIKE "MEW"—how purrfect!

99

PECULIAR PLACE-NAMES

Study any map and you'll know that some place-names sound funnier than others, but are these too unbelievable to be TRUE? Some of them are! Can you figure out WHICH ONES?

1 MUGGLESVILLE, U.K.

2 A.-O.K., U.S.A.

3 CHOCOLATE, BOLIVIA

4 WICKY WACKY, AUSTRALIA

5 FLUSHING, NETHERLANDS

6 BOO BOO, BOTSWANA

7 BANANARAMA, PALAU

8 ZIGZAG, U.S.A.

9 MONKEY'S UNCLE, CAMBODIA

10 POOP, MEXICO

11 OGRE, LATVIA

12 MOOSE JAW, CANADA

PADDLING
FOR PROOF

REAL OR FAKE?

Would you sail across the Pacific Ocean to prove a point? For years, no one was quite sure how the U.S. islands of Hawaii were settled. When historians suggested the people came from Polynesia, thousands of miles away, many claimed it was an impossible feat. So, the historians set out to prove it. In 1976, a small crew hopped aboard a 60-foot (18-m) boat much like those used some 1,500 years ago by Polynesian seafaring explorers. Without an engine and navigating only by the stars, the crew of native Hawaiians and scientists wanted to show that those ancient people were fully capable of crossing thousands of miles of open ocean. And the crew proved naysayers wrong when after 34 days of sailing and paddling by the stars, they pulled into a Tahitian harbor more than 2,000 miles (3,200 km) away. A few years later, the boat set out on another expedition, making the return journey, showing that a round-trip by ancient Polynesians had indeed been possible.

FUN FACT

Since *HŌKŪLEʻA* was built, she's sailed more than 26,000 miles (41,840 km)!

REAL

HONEST
ABE

THE POLYNESIAN VOYAGING SOCIETY RE-CREATED THE PACIFIC CROSSING IN THEIR CUSTOM-BUILT BOAT, *HŌKŪLE'A* (HO-KOO-LAY-AH). Its design, basically two big canoes held side by side with rope, was based on old drawings and descriptions of ancient Polynesian boats. To navigate without the aid of any modern technology, the crew recruited a man named Mau Piailug from a tiny, remote Micronesian island. He taught them how to use not only the stars but also other clues in nature to navigate.

SPOOKY SPOTLIGHT FROM SPACE

Since September 2016, a mysterious giant spotlight has been shining on the small town of Marfa, Texas, U.S.A.—and it might be from aliens! City officials first thought it was a malfunctioning satellite. The orbiting spacecraft are sometimes used to track the movements of endangered rams across the region. But a quick check with space agencies showed no satellites near the city's airspace. The curious situation then came to the attention of international space officials, who held a secret meeting to discuss who or what might be beaming the light. The best way to find out, they decided: Send astronauts from the International Space Station to investigate. A select few are now training to fly a smaller spacecraft to the spot where the light seems to be coming from and approach any questionable object they see. The people of Marfa can hardly wait—they haven't seen the stars since this started!

FAKE!

LITTLE
WHITE LIE

A NONSTOP SPOTLIGHT SHINING FROM SPACE ONTO A CITY WOULD BE A BIG DEAL, AND SOMETHING YOU WOULD HAVE HEARD OF. Still, there's never a shortage of alien stories and people who want to believe them. The National UFO Reporting Center, based in Davenport, Washington, U.S.A., keeps track of alien sightings. Its data shows the state of California has the most claims: 12,500 and counting. Texas comes in fourth, with more than 4,500.

108

IDENTIFY THE LIE!

For each question group below, two statements are TRUE, and one is FALSE. Can you put your finger on the fib?

1

A. Zebras' black and white stripes aren't just for looks—they also keep the African animals cool!

B. Scientists discovered a species of frog that looks just like Kermit the Frog.

C. An American teenager invented earmuffs, in 1873.

2

A. The moon has Wi-Fi. You could stream a show online there!

B. A toilet wasn't shown in an American film until 1960.

C. The human brain is 30 percent fat.

ANSWERS: 1. A: Scientists have speculated for centuries about why zebras are striped. Recent studies found that the stripes act as a bug repellent! The black and white stripes—the narrower the better—confuse biting flies by making it harder for the insects to see the African animals. 2. C: A person's brain is actually twice as fatty—60 percent! Because the average human brain weighs about three pounds (1.4 kg), that's nearly two pounds (0.9 kg) of fat you're carrying around in your noggin!

ANCIENT GREEKS ROCKED THE VOTE

REAL OR FAKE?

People today who use paper or computers to cast their votes may be amused to hear how the ancient Greeks cast theirs—by placing pebbles in jars! Two urns, which are basically large vases with lids, were designated to represent two different options. People then placed their pebble in the urn of their choice. Someone would count the pebbles and whichever urn, or option, had the most, won. The process could have kept voters' preferences somewhat secret: Pebbles mostly look alike, so there was no way to tell by looking at a stone who put it there. But bystanders may have watched who walked to which urn, historians say. Another problem, possibly: People sneaking pebbles into and out of urns. It wasn't a perfect process, but at more than 2,500 years old, it's one of the oldest known examples of voting.

HONEST
ABE

REAL

FUN FACT

Morris the cat once ran for mayor of the Mexican city of Xalapa. One of his campaign promises was TO DONATE LEFTOVER KITTY LITTER TO FILL POTHOLES IN THE STREETS.

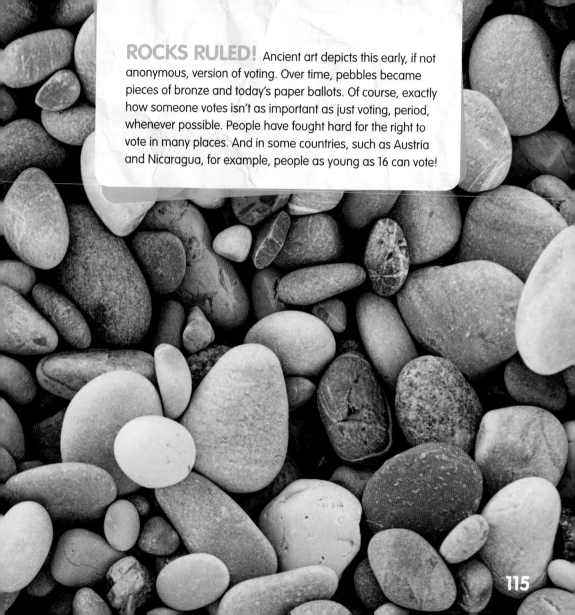

ROCKS RULED! Ancient art depicts this early, if not anonymous, version of voting. Over time, pebbles became pieces of bronze and today's paper ballots. Of course, exactly how someone votes isn't as important as just voting, period, whenever possible. People have fought hard for the right to vote in many places. And in some countries, such as Austria and Nicaragua, for example, people as young as 16 can vote!

ARTISTS GO
FOR THE GOLD

Have you ever heard of an Olympian who won a medal for music? From 1912 to 1948, this feat was possible because artists—not just athletes—competed in the Olympics! Categories of the fine art Olympics included architecture, painting, literature, and sculpture, in addition to music. All entries had to be inspired by sports, but only some were displayed in museums during the Olympics. The medal system was sometimes strange: Judges gave out only a silver medal for a category, no gold or bronze. Or no medals were awarded at all. If you've never heard of the artistic Olympics before, it's because the International Olympic Committee rarely mentions the past practice. In fact, all medals awarded for fine arts have been removed from countries' official medal counts!

REAL

HONEST
ABE

IN 2002, THE BOOK *THE FORGOTTEN OLYMPIC ART COMPETITIONS* WAS PUBLISHED, SHEDDING SOME LIGHT ON THIS LITTLE-KNOWN FACT. Though the first modern Olympics were held in 1896, in Athens, Greece, the art competitions weren't added until 16 years later. International Olympic Committee founder Baron Pierre de Coubertin pushed for their inclusion, and in 1912 not only got his way but also won the gold medal in literature (he submitted his entry under a fake name)!

PEPPY POOCHES
CHEER

Dogs are natural-born cheerleaders. They're full of energy and excitement, adore audiences, and pep people up. So it was only a matter of time before someone created the cutest sport ever: dog cheering! Competitions were first held in Anaheim, California, in 2003 and have since spread to 11 other states, for a total of 57 teams. Each team has a captain (a person, not a pooch) who teaches 10 dogs tricks typically performed by human cheerleaders. These include cartwheels and back handsprings as well as crowd-pleasers like the basket toss, in which two dogs on their hind legs use their forelegs to toss another dog 20 feet (6 m) high in the air before catching it. Just like the real thing, routines are set to music. And the peppy pups wear matching skirts and tops, and, when possible, even pull their fur into a ponytail!

FAKE!

DOG CHEERING DOESN'T EXIST. The list of tricks was meant to tip you off: Dogs definitely aren't able to do cartwheels, much less a basket toss! But dogs have been performing for people for a long time, in everything from breeders' competitions to dog dancing competitions. So a less complex form of dog cheering may be in the not-too-distant future!

123

SILLY SLANG
SWEEPS NATIONS

Some slang is just plain silly. Like Australians' "fair dinkum," which means "genuine," or Americans' "on fleek," which means "on point." But in 2016, a really ridiculous new slang swept North America, becoming so popular that the *Oxford English Dictionary* included it in its 2017 edition. So what's the word? It's two, "erp merped," and it means to finish something. Kids everywhere from Toronto, Canada, to Cancún, Mexico, were answering "I erp merped it" when their parents asked if they'd finished their homework. A pop star made up a silly song about the slang that went viral. Millions of people shared their favorite ways to use the slang on social media. And in Texas, a group of teens created a dance move named after it: A person opens their arms wide while saying "erp" and then closes them while saying "merped." Say what?!

FAKE!

LITTLE WHITE LIE

ALTHOUGH "ERP MERPED" ISN'T REAL, PEOPLE WERE SAYING A LOT OF OTHER SILLY THINGS IN 2016. That year, the *Oxford English Dictionary* added the following funny slang to its online dictionary: YOLO (short for the saying "You only live once"), kayfabe (a noun for planned performances that are presented as being spontaneous), and squee (an exclamation to show excitement).

COW BACKPACKS
CATCH BURPS

REAL OR FAKE?

Cow burps are a big problem. It's not their smell; it's the fact that they pollute the planet. In the United States alone, roughly 20 percent of methane, a greenhouse gas that causes global warming, comes from cow burps (their toots contribute some, too, but not as much). So scientists have been studying ways to reduce how much cow gas gets into the air. One idea out of Argentina is so weird it made world news: Make cows wear backpacks! A big plastic bag strapped atop a cow collects gas from its tummy via a carefully inserted tube. It sounds silly, but it works: The contraption captures about 1,200 liters of gas from each cow every day. Of that, 250 to 300 liters are methane. Scientists say that gas can be turned into an energy source strong enough to power a refrigerator for a full day!

HONEST ABE

REAL

SCIENTISTS HAVE BEEN PUTTING BACKPACKS ON COWS IN ARGENTINA FOR ALMOST A DECADE, AS A WAY TO REDUCE THE AMOUNT OF METHANE THAT ESCAPES FROM THEIR MOUTHS. Although it works, the practice isn't widespread. Scientists are still studying other ways to curb cow methane, such as tweaking the animals' diet.

THE CASE OF
THE MYSTERIOUS
MOUNDS

Scientists working in South America say they have finally cracked a really weird case: Who or what has been making mysterious six-foot (2-m)-tall mounds sprinkled across **Venezuela and Colombia.** Each human-size bump is covered in vegetation and surrounded by water-filled ditches, in a remote swath of wetland roughly the size of Ireland. Guesses of who built the lumps have ranged from aliens to ancient peoples, but the answer is something much smaller: earthworms. The little wrigglers didn't haul mini-mounds of dirt on their backs or in their mouths to build the structures, though. Instead, surrounded by water, they simply stayed put and pooped. And pooped. And pooped. Yep, the mounds are made not of dirt, but of worm doo-doo!

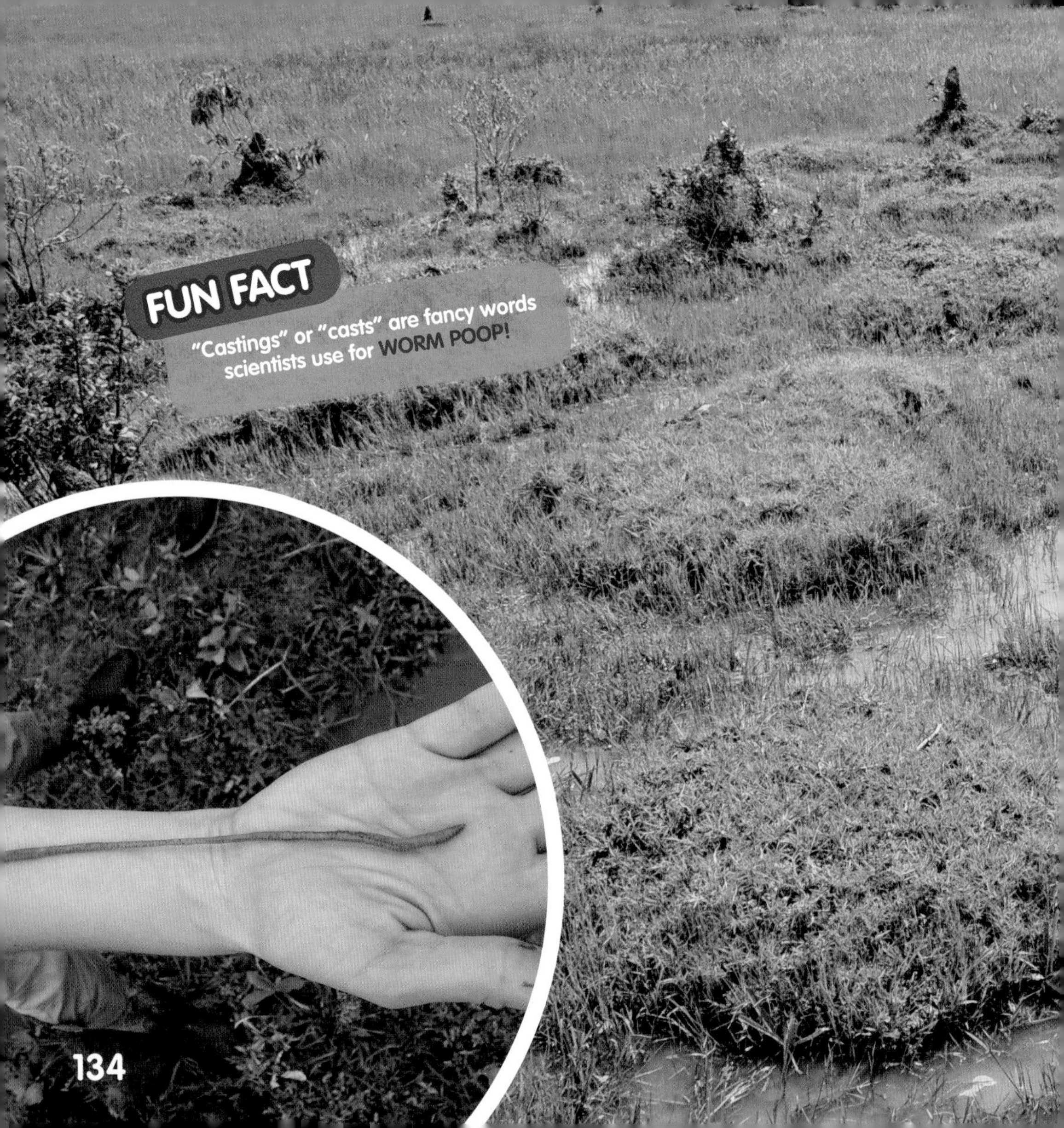

FUN FACT

"Castings" or "casts" are fancy words scientists use for **WORM POOP!**

REAL

HONEST ABE

THE MOUNDS, CALLED *SURALES*, REALLY ARE FORMED FROM EARTHWORM FECES! An international team of scientists made the announcement in 2016 after studying the towers and determining the worms most likely made them. Finding the remote, little-studied structures was half the battle, the team said. They had to rely on old books and Google Earth just to pinpoint the piles' locations.

ONLINE PIG-OUTS
PAY BIG BUCKS

There's a new type of Internet celebrity in Korea. And all the online star has to do is eat a lot and loudly while live streaming the meal for fans at home to watch. The funny food fad earns some eaters so much money they don't have to work regular jobs. People who tune in to watch the eaters reward big portions—think enough food for a family of six!—and noisy slurping and crunching with virtual balloons. The eaters can then exchange those for real money. Eaters can also bring in the balloon-bucks by describing in detail how spicy or delicious something is or how full they feel and providing entertainment during the meal, such as doing a little dance. There are thousands of eaters, and the most watched have some 10,000 fans each, so those balloons can add up!

REAL

HONEST
ABE

THIS PECULIAR PRACTICE STARTED IN 2013 AND HAS SINCE SPREAD ALL OVER THE WORLD. Eaters now gobble up everything from Korean cuisine to vegan dinners. And they often invite friends and family to join them at the table. Why is the peculiar practice so popular? Some fans say tuning in beats eating alone at home.

MANSIONS
FOR THE BIRDS

Birds don't have arms, but they can still build some seriously mighty mansions! In Australia and on the island of New Guinea, bowerbirds build structures about nine feet (3 m) tall and decorate them with everything from potato chip bags, glittering jewelry, and flowers to tiny toys, snail shells, and even shiny, dead insects! These artistic animals find anything they can grab in the forest and use them to spruce up their twig-based buildings. The bigger and shinier and more elaborate, the better! That's because these structures aren't nests. They're called bowers (hence the birds' names), and males build them to attract females. The birds pull out all the stops—even making a mixture of charcoal dust, plant juice, and saliva that they hold in their beaks and paint their bower's walls with! All this adds up to one beautiful bower.

REAL

HONEST
ABE

BOWERS NEED TO BE SEEN TO BE BELIEVED! Not only are the structures awesome examples of avian architecture, they're also stages for amazing acts. Bowerbirds perform impressive song-and-dance routines there, making the animals triple-threat artists that could give any pop star a run for their money!

MORE AMAZING STRUCTURES
BUILT BY ANIMALS

Animals can create things that are huge, complex, and even artistic. Can you tell which of these amazing animal feats are REAL?

1 A 100-POUND (45-KG) BEEHIVE WAS REMOVED FROM AN ORLANDO, FLORIDA, U.S.A., HOME IN 2015.

2 THE MOST MASSIVE BEAVER DAM IN THE WORLD IS MORE THAN HALF A MILE (.85 KM) LONG.

3 THE LARGEST PRAIRIE DOG TOWN SPANNED 25,000 SQUARE MILES (64,750 SQ KM).

4 THE BIGGEST BIRD NEST IN THE WORLD WAS BUILT BY BALD EAGLES AND MEASURED MORE THAN 9 FEET (2.7 M) ACROSS AND 20 FEET (6 M) DEEP.

5 A TROOP OF MONKEYS PAINTED A MURAL OF A BANANA FOREST ONTO A WALL IN NEW DELHI, INDIA.

6 MYSTERIOUS, THREE-FOOT (1-M)-HIGH MOUNDS FOUND ON EVERY CONTINENT EXCEPT ANTARCTICA WERE LIKELY FORMED BY GOPHERS OVER HUNDREDS OF YEARS, SCIENTISTS SAY.

ANSWERS: 1. Real; 2. Real; 3. Real; 4. Real; 5. Fake; 6. Real

ALASKA
ICE MONSTER

Is there a slippery monster hiding in Alaska, U.S.A.'s remote waters? Thousands of people were left wondering just that after watching a video posted to the social media site of the state's Bureau of Land Management. On October 26, 2016, the government organization shared a short but scary-looking video of the icy Chena River. The caption read: "#WildWednesday Our Fairbanks employees captured this strange 'thing' swimming in the Chena River in Fairbanks, #Alaska." In the clip, a large, snake-like object appears to slowly wriggle through the wintery water. People and news media all over the world shared the video of the Alaska "ice monster" and speculated what the creepy creature could be. It didn't appear to be any known animal, and—even more alarming—a government employee had posted the video, so it must be a real-life monster sighting!

147

FAKE!

LITTLE WHITE LIE

FUN FACT

Alhough the iconic photo of SCOTLAND'S LOCH NESS MONSTER first appeared in the 1930s, the legend of the lake monster stretches all the way back to the sixth century!

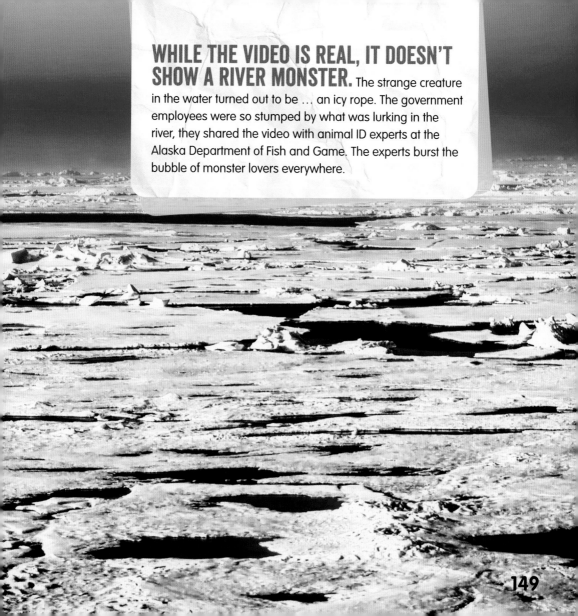

WHILE THE VIDEO IS REAL, IT DOESN'T SHOW A RIVER MONSTER. The strange creature in the water turned out to be … an icy rope. The government employees were so stumped by what was lurking in the river, they shared the video with animal ID experts at the Alaska Department of Fish and Game. The experts burst the bubble of monster lovers everywhere.

MOUNTIES TO RIDE MOOSE
INSTEAD OF HORSES

REAL OR FAKE?

The Royal Canadian Mounted Police are famous for keeping the peace while wearing bright red uniforms and sitting atop horses. But starting in 2020, the Mounties, as they're called, will stop riding horses and instead sit astride moose! While the switch shocked many, it made sense for two reasons, Canadian officials said. Horses have a harder time withstanding the cold than moose do. And moose are a better national symbol, because they're native to Canada and live throughout the country. But first police have to figure out how to train moose to let people ride them. That's no easy task: The animals are reclusive, wild, and strong. But the Mounties have a plan: Since 2016, a dozen officers have been living on a remote island that's home to 22 moose in an effort to get the animals used to giving rides (and tickets!).

There's a famous photo of U.S. PRESIDENT THEODORE ROOSEVELT RIDING A MOOSE—but it's fake. Experts say he was actually riding a horse and someone manipulated two images to make it appear as though he were atop a moose.

152

THE MOUNTIES AREN'T FORGOING HORSES FOR MOOSE.

It would be really hard to get a moose to let someone ride it; they don't like that. A lot of people wouldn't like that, either, because the animals are wildlife, not domestic animals. But most Mounties don't even ride horses anymore, anyway, or wear the bright red uniforms on a daily basis. The animals and outfit are used mostly for ceremonial purposes today.

LITTLE WHITE LIE

FAKE!

SCIENTISTS DISCOVER
ITCH TRICK

REAL OR FAKE?

Having an itch you can't scratch is the worst! But scientists say they've found a surprising solution for people plagued with poison ivy and other itchy ailments. A study found that scratching the non-itchy, opposite limb while using a mirror to make it look like it's the itchy limb fools the brain into thinking the itch was scratched! The trick, which is simple enough to do at home, works like this: A mirror is placed between an itchy person's arms, and they're asked to look into it so that they can't see their itchy arm but instead only a reflection of the non-itchy one. Then someone else scratches the non-itchy arm (the trick won't work if the itchy person does the scratching). Participants reported feeling relief when scientists performed the trick on them. Being fooled never felt so good!

REAL

HONEST
ABE

A TEAM OF SCIENTISTS IN GERMANY PUBLISHED A STUDY ABOUT THIS ITCH TRICK IN 2013. It really works, though not as well as actually scratching the itchy arm, the participants reported. For their work, the scientists were given the 2016 Ig Nobel Prize in Medicine. The Ig Nobels award silly-sounding research, such as the scientist who put little pants on rats and the scientist who dressed up and acted like a goat (also 2016 Ig Nobel winners). Their work gives new meaning to the saying "in the name of science"!

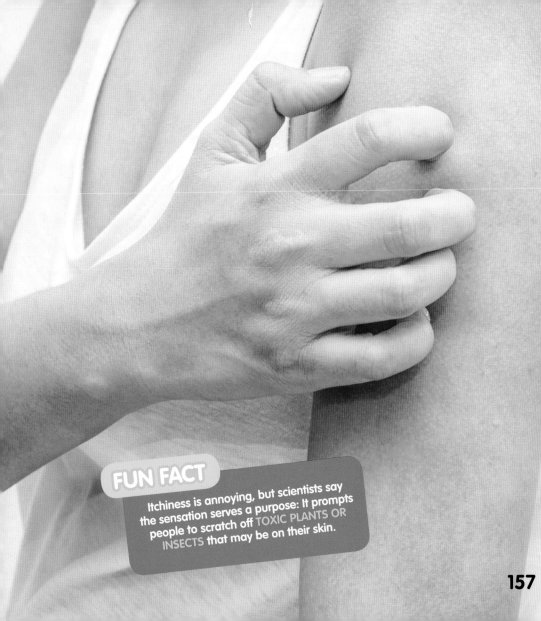

Itchiness is annoying, but scientists say the sensation serves a purpose: It prompts people to scratch off TOXIC PLANTS OR INSECTS that may be on their skin.

REAL OR FAKE?

MORE IG NOBEL AWARD WINNERS

The IG NOBEL AWARDS reward studies that are odd or silly but still contribute to science. Can you guess which of the following studies were actually done in the name of science?

1 Observed cows to see how long they lie down before standing up, and vice versa

158

2 Shot volunteers in the hand with a laser beam while they looked at ugly and pretty paintings

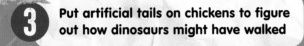

3 Put artificial tails on chickens to figure out how dinosaurs might have walked

4 Disguised people as polar bears to see how reindeer reacted to them

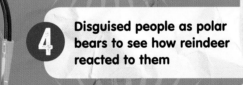

5 Made mice listen to opera music

ANSWERS: Real! All of these are real! Fake: None!

MICHELANGELO
MADE UGLY ART!

Italian Renaissance artist Michelangelo has been famous for 500 years. He carved the "David" statue and painted the ceiling of the Sistine Chapel, among other masterpieces. But he also created smaller, more simple pieces of art, such as "Ball and Boy," a painting of a sloppily drawn circle next to a stick figure. Never heard of it? That's because, art experts agree, it stinks. Really stinks. As does all of the art Michelangelo created after about age 30. His work later in life consists mostly of crudely drawn stick figures and basic shapes in black and white. Art historians aren't sure why Michelangelo abandoned his earlier approach to art. Some speculate he wore himself out creating so many masterpieces in such a short amount of time. If you're curious to see Michelangelo's ugly art in person, you're out of luck: No gallery or museum has displayed it in almost 100 years.

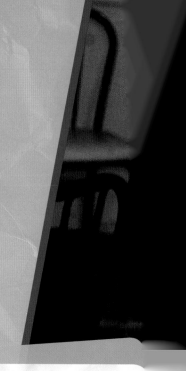

BIG OL' WHOPPER

FAKE!

MICHELANGELO WAS A WELL-RESPECTED ARTIST UNTIL HE DIED AT AGE 88 IN 1564. He was carving his last (and not ugly!) sculpture when he was just a few weeks shy of his 89th birthday. There is, however, a home for really ugly art, whoever made it. The Museum of Bad Art is an online gallery of the world's worst art. Some of the pieces can even be viewed in person at two galleries in Massachusetts, U.S.A.

FAKE NEWS
BEATS REAL NEWS

When it comes to picking a president, people often rely on the news to give them the straight scoop. But on one of the world's biggest social media sites, the top fake news stories about the 2016 U.S. presidential election were more popular than the real ones! People using the site shared and commented on more of the fake election stories than the real ones for the three months leading up to Election Day. The fakes racked up more than eight million shares, comments, and other reader feedback. The real deals?: A little more than seven million. Fake stories came from hoax sites and blogs and made false claims that may have impacted the outcome of the election.

REAL

HONEST
ABE

FAKE U.S. ELECTION STORIES REALLY DID BEAT OUT REAL ONES ON THE SUPERSIZE SOCIAL MEDIA SITE IN LATE 2016. The disturbing discovery was made by a popular news website about a week after Election Day in the United States. The most popular fake story was an article claiming that the pope endorsed one of the candidates. Interestingly, the real stories outperformed the fake ones up until those final three months before Election Day. The lesson for readers: Always check news sources before sharing!

167

SPOT THE FAKE!

Do you have the eye of a spy? See if you can tell which of these photos are REAL and which are really FAKE!

Heads up!: A leaping whale made a really big splash at a surfing competition.

1

A giraffe's superlong neck helps it better balance atop a rope across a preserve in Africa.

2

SPOT THE FAKE!

1

Practice makes perfect. It better, when you're on the edge of a cliff!

Video calls aren't just for people—monkeys make them, too, though they spend most of the time making faces at each other.

2

171

YOGA GOES
TO THE GOATS

Have you ever wished your yoga class allowed goats? In 2016, an Oregon, U.S.A., farm announced a new offering: a yoga class where goats were welcome, too. Billies and nannies are allowed to wander among people in pretzel-like poses, poop on yoga mats, or bleat, snort, and lick people while they contemplate their place in the universe. The farm got the idea after hosting an outdoor yoga class that a few goats crashed. Participants loved it, so the farm started regularly offering Goat Yoga, with about half a dozen of the animals. Its waiting list grew to hundreds of eager yogis. And as word of the wacky class spread, it made headlines all over and even inspired other yoga-with-goats classes elsewhere. If this trend continues, the pose "down dog" may need to be renamed "down goat"!

REAL

HONEST
ABE

IT'S TRUE! NO REGRETS FARM, IN ALBANY, OREGON, REALLY DOES HOLD GOAT YOGA CLASSES. They might sound silly, but the idea behind them is sweet, says the farm's owner: to bring joy and comfort to people. Bonus: Chickens and a cat also join in!

VIKINGS SAILED
THE U.S. SOUTH

A team of trash collectors in Tennessee, U.S.A., rewrote history in 2014 when they stumbled upon something special. Half-buried in the banks of the Mississippi River was an ancient Viking ship! The fearsome seafaring people from northern Europe arrived on North America's shores some 1,000 years ago. Historians thought the colonists had stuck to Canada's coastline. But the boat's discovery deep in the U.S. South shows the Vikings traveled more than 2,500 miles (4,000 km) into the continent's interior. A team of scientists from the nearby University of Memphis inspected the boat on-site and reported it was 52 feet (16 m) long, held 20 to 30 people, and could sail up to 75 miles (121 km) a day. What's more, they said, the ship could be evidence that a vast colony called Vinland mentioned in Viking myths could be real!

FAKE!

BIG OL' WHOPPER

THIS NEWS STORY HAS CIRCULATED SINCE 2014, BUT IT'S A HOAX FIRST PUBLISHED BY A SATIRICAL NEWS WEBSITE KNOWN FOR ITS FAKE STORIES. Those who believed the story may have been so excited about it that they didn't see the site's disclaimer. The lesson: Make sure a site's stories are accurate before believing and sharing them!

As of 2016, there is only one confirmed Viking site in all of North America: L'Anse aux Meadows, on Canada's Newfoundland island. It's evidence that the Vikings reached the New World about 500 YEARS BEFORE CHRISTOPHER COLUMBUS.

ONE-OF-A-KIND
OUTFIT

Do you ever go shopping and can't find what you're looking for? One company offers a solution that sounds too good to be true: Draw your own outfit! First, print out a dress or T-shirt template from the company's website. Next, draw whatever you want on it, in whatever colors you like. It could feature your favorite pet, aliens in space, your best friend, monkeys with pizza for eyes—anything! And you can include stickers and other pasted-on items. When you're done, take a photo of your art and upload it to the website. Then wait for your one-of-a-kind, ready-to-wear creation to arrive at your house. When people ask where your outfit came from, you can say "My mind!"

182

REAL

THE CLOTHING COMPANY, PICTURE THIS, LAUNCHED IN SUMMER 2016, AND THE ORDERS STARTED POURING IN. It even offers custom-made doll-size dresses! The inspiration for the company came from one of the co-founders' kids, who rocked a dress featuring her drawing and sewn by her mom!

SOARING TEMPERATURES
SET FECES AFLAME

n July 2016, residents of tiny Throop, New York, U.S.A., called state officials to complain about a foul odor in the air. An investigation was opened and the cause quickly identified: a heap of horse poop outside a local stable had been set on fire. Who would do such a nasty thing? The sun, it turns out. Scientists say the local weather had gotten so hot and dry that the poopy pile climbed to a temperature high enough to ignite on its own. That may sound fishy. But the freak accident wasn't a first for the stable owners. They say the poop had previously caught fire on its own, but in those instances the wind had wafted the stench away from town.

185

REAL

HONEST
ABE

CALLED SPONTANEOUS COMBUSTION, THIS PHENOMENON CAN HAPPEN WHEN ORGANIC (LIVING OR ONCE LIVING) MATERIAL GETS DRY AND HOT ENOUGH, BETWEEN 300 AND 400°F (150 AND 200°C). The middle of a big pile of manure—a good but dirty fuel—can reach these temperatures in the right conditions. And then: *kaboom!*

CITY GETS
SNEAKY SIDEWALKS

REAL OR FAKE?

St. Petersburg, Russia, is serious about keeping its public places clean. As of 2018, it's illegal to spit gum onto the city's sidewalks and streets. Nobody likes stepping in the stuff. But in 2015, the mayor got into a particularly sticky situation: While walking in a parade, she stepped on a glob and in an effort to get it off her shoe got it all over her hands and then in her hair. Worse: The embarrassing ordeal was recorded and went viral. Not long after, she announced the new law. And, as important, how the city would enforce it: By coating streets and sidewalks with a special paint that sends spit-out gum bouncing back at offenders! Amazingly, the paint can recognize gum's unique chemical makeup and stiffen when the stuff hits it, so that the wad won't stick. That way, it repels only gum—and those who spit it out!

FAKE!

LITTLE WHITE LIE

FUN FACT

In 2004, SINGAPORE allowed citizens to buy gum again—but only from pharmacists for health purposes!

THIS SILLY STORY IS MADE-UP, BUT IT WAS INSPIRED BY A FEW FACTS! For starters, it's illegal to spit anything onto sidewalks and streets in Singapore. And the country banned the sale of gum in 1992, though it's still legal to chew it. And San Francisco, California, U.S.A., and Hamburg, Germany, have coated some city walls with a paint that makes pee splash back. It repels other liquids, too, though, so watch where you spill things in those cities!

190

DOLPHIN WINS GAME SHOW

Have you ever met a millionaire dolphin? In 2007, a supersmart dolphin named Einstein competed on the popular TV game show *Who Wants to Be a Millionaire* and won! Einstein beat out two other contestants—both people—by using his nose to nudge his chosen answers to eight trivia questions. Then, in the final round, he correctly answered the question "Where is Paddington Bear originally from?" (answer: Peru), winning one million dollars. While confetti rained down and amazed audience members stood and clapped, Einstein let out a high-pitched, perhaps victorious, whistle. His owner says she didn't train him to play the game, but noted he has appeared in over a dozen commercials, and has shown "exceptional intelligence," according to animal behavior experts. So what does a dolphin do with a million dollars? Donates it to ocean conservation, of course!

one million

34 3434 34

FEBRUARY 3, 2003**

$ 1,000,000.00

0145870076

FAKE!

LITTLE
WHITE LIE

NO DOLPHIN HAS EVER WON A GAME SHOW, MUCH LESS REALLY PARTICIPATED IN ONE. Scientists agree dolphins are smart, but not so smart that they could consistently answer trivia questions correctly. Scientists do often use games, though, to study animal brains. In one famous experiment from the 1990s, pigs learned how to play (simple) video games!

195

STRANGE STORY OF
WORLD'S PUNIEST PARK

REAL OR FAKE?

The world's smallest park certainly doesn't look like one. Mill Ends Park, in downtown Portland, Oregon, U.S.A., sits in the middle of a busy street, surrounded by a concrete ring, and is a mere two feet (0.6 m) across. The puny park may also be the world's strangest. Its fans say it's home to the only leprechaun colony outside Ireland. And it's also been home to a tiny swimming pool and diving board—for butterflies, of course—and a miniature Ferris wheel. Toy dinosaurs, little green army men, and tiny UFOs have dotted its dirt, placed there by passersby. You would think only one person at a time could appreciate such a small spot. But concerts, picnics, and parties—especially in celebration of St. Patrick's Day—are regularly held there. And, in 2013, it was the scene of a crime that made national news: Its lone tree was stolen. This tiny park packs in a lot of action!

REAL

HONEST
ABE

THE LEPRECHAUNS ARE FAKE, BUT THE PARK IS REAL! Mill Ends became an official city park in 1976, three decades after a journalist who worked nearby, Dick Fagan, created the kooky park. The empty hole in the middle of a median had been intended for a lamppost. But it never showed up, so Fagan filled it with dirt and flowers and the rest is history!

FUN FACT

Fagan claimed to be the only person who could see the park's head leprechaun, PATRICK O'TOOLE.

SAVE OUR PARK

MORE SUPERSMALL SPACES

A tiny place can still be a really big deal. Can you guess which of the following are REAL and which are little LIES?

1 The world's smallest restaurant, in Vacone, Italy, has only one table with two seats.

2 London's smallest library is housed inside a red telephone booth.

3 Oregon's D River is only 120 feet (37 m) long.

4 Vatican City, at just .17 square mile (.44 sq km), is the world's smallest country.

5 The world's smallest zoo, in Portugal, is home to only one animal: a flea.

6 A shoe store the size of an elevator, in Taiwan, sells just one pair of shoes at a time.

BUFORD
POP 1
ELEV 8000

7 The tiny town of Buford, Wyoming, U.S.A., has a population of one.

ANSWERS: 1. True; 2. True; 3. True; 4. True; 5. True; 6. False; 7. True

INDEX

Illustrations are indicated by **boldface.**

CREDITS

All interior artwork by Tom Nick Cocotos unless otherwise noted below.

Cover (front and back), Tom Nick Cocotos; 4 (LO), nevodka/Shutterstock; 5 (LO RT), shalamov/Getty Images; 6 (LO RT), Javier Brosch/Shutterstock; 6-7, Olga Popova/Shutterstock; 7 (CTR RT), Wild Horizon/Getty Images; 10-11, LeoPatrizi/Getty Images; 14-15, TJ Roth/Sipa USA; 18-19, Olga Popova/Shutterstock; 20 (LO LE), Roninphotography/Dreamstime; 20 (LO RT), Eric Isselee/Shutterstock; 20 (LO CTR), Mtsaride/Shutterstock; 21 (UP LE), Tatiana Popova/Shutterstock; 21 (UP CTR), bloomua/Shutterstock; 21 (LO), Evikka/Shutterstock; 21 (LO), photka/Shutterstock; 21 (UP RT), Hugo Felix/Shutterstock; 21 (LO RT), Stockforlife/Shutterstock; 24-25, Xinhua/Alamy; 28-29, Kim Karpeles/Alamy; 30, Maynard Case/Shutterstock; 30 (LE), Skypixel/Dreamstime; 31 (LO LE), Kuttelvaserova Stuchelova/Shutterstock; 31 (UP), Chones/Shutterstock; 31 (RT), nevodka/Shutterstock; 34-35, ChiccoDodiFC/Shutterstock; 36, Alexander Demianchuk/Reuters; 37, Gandee Vasan/Getty Images; 38, Ilya Naymushin/Reuters; 39, John Lund/Getty Images; 42-43, shalamov/Getty Images; 44, Acambium64/Shutterstock; 44, Yuganov Konstantin/Shutterstock; 44 (RT), AlenKadr/Shutterstock; 45 (RT), Four Oaks/Shutterstock; 45 (LO LE), Ermolaev Alexander/Shutterstock; 45, PhilAugustavo/Getty Images; 48-49, Carolyn Hampton; 52 (LE), PhilAugustavo/Getty Images; 52-52 (UP), Peangdao/Shutterstock; 53, Olga Popova/Shutterstock; 54 (UP RT), Ben Molyneux/Alamy; 54 (LO), Obak/Shutterstock; 54 (LO LE), Africa Studio/Shutterstock; 55 (UP), Evikka/Shutterstock; 55 (CTR LE), Eldad Carin/iStock; 55 (LO RT), Mazzzur/Shutterstock; 58-59, Nick Measures/Getty Images; 62-63, Vadim Sadovski/Shutterstock; 66-67, dpa picture alliance/Alamy; 68, Joseph Sohm/Shutterstock; 68, David Franklin/Shutterstock; 68 (UP RT), JasonOndreicka/Getty Images; 69 (CTR RT), Art_man/Shutterstock; 69 (LE), Odua Images/Shutterstock; 72-73, Otto Rogge/Getty Images; 72, Accent/Shutterstock; 76-77, Josep Lago/AFP/Getty Images; 80-81, Ricardo Reitmeyer/Shutterstock; 84-85, Jason Lindsey/Alamy; 86, Jagdeep Rajput; 87, James D. Morgan/REX/Shutterstock; 88, A. Witte/C. Mahaney/Getty Images; 89, Joe Pepler/REX/Shutterstock; 90, Tim Fitzharris/Minden Pictures; 91, Lucas Jackson/Reuters; 94-95, Paradise Picture/Shutterstock; 98-99, Christina Balit; 100-101, Koncz/Shutterstock; 100-101, Dja65/Shutterstock; 104-105, Hugh Gentry/Reuters; 108-109, Igor Zh./Shutterstock; 110, Evgenia Bolyukh/Shutterstock; 110, prapass/Shutterstock; 111 (UP), godrick/Shutterstock; 111 (CTR LE), Somchai Som/Shutterstock; 111 (LO RT), Kts/Dreamstime; 114-115, vvvita/Dreamstime; 114-115, Olympic Museum Lausanne; 122-123, John Lund/Getty Images; 126-127, peshkov/Getty Images; 130-131, Marcos Brindicci/Reuters; 134-135, Doyle McKey; 134-135, Doyle McKey; 138-139, kazoka30/Getty Images; 142-143, Konrad Wothe/Minden Pictures; 144 (LO LE), Eric Isselee/Shutterstock; 144-145 (CTR), Anat Chant/Shutterstock; 145 (UP RT), S.R. Maglione/Shutterstock; 148-149, Maksimilian/Shutterstock; 152-153, Mark Spowart/Alamy; 156-157, namtipStudio/Shutterstock; 158-159 (LO LE), Dieter Hawlan/Shutterstock; 159 (UP LE), Valentina_S/Shutterstock; 159 (UP), Catmando/Shutterstock; 159 (LO), Rudmer Zwerver/Shutterstock; 159 (LO LE), docent/Shutterstock; 159 (RT), Iakov Filimonov/Shutterstock; 162-163 (RT), Brian Cahn/Zuma Wire; 166-167, Franco Origlia/Getty Images; 168, David Gray/Reuters; 169, Sergey Nivens/Shutterstock; 170, VCG/VCG via Getty Images; 171, Wiratchai wansamngam/Shutterstock; 174-175, Lainey Morse; 178-179, Sylphe_7/Getty Images; 182-183 (All), Picture This Clothing; 186-187, dinozzaver/Shutterstock; 190-191, Africa Studio/Shutterstock; 194-195, Mike Hill/Getty Images; 198-199, AP Photo/Don Ryan; 200 (UP), smartin69/Getty Images; 201 (UP), Mariia Golovianko/Shutterstock201 (LO), dschreiber29/Getty Images201 (RT), Borislav Bajkic/Dreamstime

206

For Sarah, who always keeps it real. —EK

Copyright © 2018 National Geographic Partners, LLC

Published by National Geographic Partners, LLC. All rights reserved. Reproduction of the whole or any part of the contents without written permission from the publisher is prohibited.

Since 1888, the National Geographic Society has funded more than 12,000 research, exploration, and preservation projects around the world. The Society receives funds from National Geographic Partners, LLC, funded in part by your purchase. A portion of the proceeds from this book supports this vital work. To learn more, visit natgeo.com/info.

NATIONAL GEOGRAPHIC and Yellow Border Design are trademarks of the National Geographic Society, used under license.

For more information, please visit nationalgeographic.com, call 1-800-647-5463, or write to the following address:

National Geographic Partners
1145 17th Street N.W.
Washington, D.C. 20036-4688 U.S.A.

Visit us online at nationalgeographic.com/books

For librarians and teachers: ngchildrensbooks.org

More for kids from National Geographic: natgeokids.com

For information about special discounts for bulk purchases, please contact National Geographic Books Special Sales: specialsales@natgeo.com

For rights or permissions inquiries, please contact National Geographic Books Subsidiary Rights: bookrights@natgeo.com

Amber Colleran, *Designer*

Trade paperback ISBN:
978-1-4263-3004-9

Reinforced library binding ISBN:
978-1-4263-3005-6

The publisher would like to thank the team who helped make this book possible: Ariane Szu-Tu, associate editor; Kathryn Robbins, art director; Shannon Hibberd, senior photo editor; Christina Ascani, associate photo editor; and Anne LeongSon and Gus Tello, production assistants.

Printed in China
17/PPS/1

WHAT IF

... you never bathed, cars drove themselves, or you could travel through time? Now that you can tell fact from fiction, try thinking about what would REALLY happen if the silly and serious scenarios in this book came true!